W9-DEO-029

WITHDRAWN
WRIGHT STATE UNIVERSITY LIBRARIES

Women in Administration

The Practicing Administrator's Leadership Series
Jerry J. Herman and Janice L. Herman, Editors

**ROADMAPS
TO SUCCESS**

Other Titles in This Series Include:

The Path to School Leadership
A Portable Mentor
Lee G. Bolman and Terrence E. Deal

Holistic Quality
Managing, Restructuring, and Empowering Schools
Jerry J. Herman

Selecting, Managing, and Marketing Technologies
Jamieson A. McKenzie

Individuals With Disabilities
Implementing the Newest Laws
Patricia F. First and Joan L. Curcio

Violence in the Schools
How to Proactively Prevent and Defuse It
Joan L. Curcio and Patricia F. First

Power Learning in the Classroom
Jamieson A. McKenzie

Conflict Resolution
Building Bridges
Neil Katz

Computers: Literacy and Learning
A Primer for Administrators
George E. Marsh II

Restructuring Schools
Doing It Right
Mike M. Milstein

Dealing With Gangs
A Handbook for Administrators
Shirley R. Lal, Dhyan Lal, and Charles M. Achilles

Women in Administration
Facilitators for Change

L. Nan Restine

CORWIN PRESS, INC.
A Sage Publications Company
Newbury Park, California

Copyright ©1993 by Corwin Press, Inc.

All rights reserved. No part of this book may be reproduced or utilized in any form or by any means, electronic or mechanical, including photocopying, recording, or by any information storage and retrieval system, without permission in writing from the publisher.

For information address:

Corwin Press, Inc.
A Sage Publications Company
2455 Teller Road
Newbury Park, California 91320

SAGE Publications Ltd.
6 Bonhill Street
London EC2A 4PU
United Kingdom

SAGE Publications India Pvt. Ltd.
M-32 Market
Greater Kailash I
New Delhi 110 048 India

Printed in the United States of America

Library of Congress Cataloging-in-Publication Data

Restine, L. Nan.
    Women in administration : facilitators for change / L. Nan
Restine.
        p.   cm. — (Roadmaps to success)
    Includes bibliographical references (p.   ).
    ISBN 0–8039–6059–X
    1. Women school administrators—United States. 2. School
management and organization—United States. 3. Educational change—
Social aspects—United States.   I. Title.   II. Series.
LB2831.82.R47   1993
371.2'0082—dc20   93–16917

93 94 95 96 10 9 8 7 6 5 4 3 2 1

Corwin Press Production Editor: Marie Louise Penchoen

Contents

Foreword

L. Nan Restine's text is true to her title. *Women in Administration: Facilitators for Change* focuses on changes that women educators can bring to schools. She talks about women as a force that can adjust to and guide change in a positive direction and that can improve our schools as one component of a broad mosaic of participants. Women are an underrepresented and underutilized group in school administration, but they are an important untapped source of experience and knowledge that should take equal part in decisions aimed at improving our schools.

Restine discusses the changes taking place in our society and in our schools as challenges to inspire and guide school improvement. She also emphasizes the need to create empowering cultures in schools through adult growth and development. The importance of effective leadership in creating the preferred future vision of schools as learning communities cannot be overstated, and the last chapter offers a definition of enlightened leadership in schools.

A unique feature in each chapter is a set of reflective questions that challenge the reader to share in the decision-making process.

JERRY J. HERMAN
JANICE L. HERMAN
Series Co-Editors

About the Author

L. Nan Restine is Assistant Professor in the Department of Educational Administration and Higher Education at Oklahoma State University. Prior to this, she was Assistant Professor of Educational Administration and Director of the Danforth Program for the Preparation of School Principals at Western Kentucky University. During that time, she consulted for the Center for Industry and Technology in the areas of Lifelong Learning and Team Building and served on a task force for site-based decision making.

She was Assistant Program Director for the Cooperative Educational Administration Internship Program, a Danforth Program, and Co-Director of AWARE at the University of New Mexico. Prior to this, she taught and held administrative positions in the public schools of New Mexico and Texas.

Restine received a B.S. from Eastern New Mexico University, an M.A. from New Mexico State University, and an Ed.S. and Ph.D. from the University of New Mexico. She has authored and co-authored books, research studies, and articles on administrator preparation, mentoring, and adult learning. Her current research interests are focused on the areas of educational administrator preparation, mentoring, and adult learning in the professions.

When we look for the contributions which contacts of peoples . . . of different races and different religions, different levels of culture . . . have made on education, we find two.

On the one hand, the emphasis has shifted from doing to the one who causes it to be done, from spontaneity to coercion, from freedom to power. With this shift has come the development of power, dry pedagogy, regimentation, indoctrination, manipulation and propaganda. These are but sorry additions . . . and they come from the insult to human life which is perpetuated whenever one human being is regarded as differentially less or more than another.

But on the other hand, out of discontinuities and rapid changes . . . has come another invention, one which perhaps would not have been born in any other setting than this one—the belief in education as an instrument for the creation of new human values.

(MARGARET MEAD, *Our Educational Emphases in Primitive Perspective*, 1943)

Introduction

"Cheshire-Puss," she began rather timidly, . . . "Would you tell me, please, which way I ought to go from here?"

"That depends a good deal on where you want to get to," said the Cat.

"I don't much care where—," said Alice.

"Then it doesn't matter which way you go," said the Cat.

(LEWIS CARROLL, *Alice's Adventures in Wonderland*)

Although the world of schools may not be as unfamiliar to us as Wonderland was to Alice, it still makes little difference which course we take if we do not have a destination. When we have a goal that matters, however, we must choose our direction. Defining where we want to go and how to get there involves exploring new ways of thinking, knowing, and behaving in the world we are familiar with.

This book is part of the series called *Roadmaps to Success* and the metaphor is fraught with meaning. Over the years, I have observed people examining their perspectives about their "roadmaps" and about what *success* means. It is instructive to observe

1

individuals and even groups as they approach solving a nine-dot puzzle—their perspectives are shown in their attempts at solution. In a similar way, almost any activity reveals how values and beliefs influence decisions. For example, when choosing a route to travel from one destination to another, some select an interstate route because of expediency, others choose secondary thoroughfares because of scenery, and others opt for flying! Still others, however few, will choose to take a detour into unexplored territories. And almost without exception, someone will ask, "What is the *correct* route (or answer)?" In the puzzle, I find that most puzzlers confine themselves by remaining within the parameters of the dots.

We learn very early and quite well how to play the game of school, to seek the answers, and to function within artificial parameters. The lessons and rules we learn in elementary school through graduate school, and beyond, remain with us and tend to shape and color our worlds. Many of those lessons and rules have changed little over the years. Yet, the world in which we live has changed. Schools are mirrors of difference and diversity beyond what is immediately observable. We could argue that even though there may be a cognitive awareness of diversity in schools, awareness alone has not resulted in dramatic shifts in the predominant models of schools and schooling. Schools remain, for the most part, symbols of our predisposition to perpetuate what has been. Thinking about schools differently means examining them for what has merit and worth and should be kept and attended to and for what should be put aside, amended, or discarded.

I borrow Roland Barth's vision of a good school as a "community of learners" (Barth, 1990) and suggest that thinking about schools as learning communities requires discarding the notions of *other*, *them*, and *those* in an effort to make the most of our collective human resources. The momentum must come from reflecting on ourselves, our assumptions, our interactions with others, and our visions of what community means.

Women in Administration: Facilitators for Change is about richness in difference and diversity. It is written for those who subscribe to the idea that schools can be better places to live and learn than many are. It does not attempt to be a cookbook with easy-to-follow recipes, nor is it aimed at a singular audience. A cookbook approach would be the antithesis of celebrating difference, given the realities of today's schools, and meaning for a singular audience would be limited. Rather, my intent is to broaden and deepen perspectives for viewing the manifestations of diversity as cultural phenomena that significantly influence our identities, values, modes of interaction, and norms of behavior. This book is about utilizing the social and professional repertoire of people in schools, and women specifically, to create positive change in schools.

Some of my own personal history and experiences will serve as a frame of reference, as will the experiences of others. I extend my appreciation to my students and colleagues, Linda Hall and Ann Horne, for allowing me to use excerpts from their educational platforms. I am convinced that we have in our schools a wealth of untapped and underutilized knowledge about people, teaching, learning, and leading. Further, I would suggest that we have tended to disregard much of what we know because of personal discomfort in stretching our minds to see other possibilities and because of the difficulty in changing certain aspects of schools. I use *difficult* because it is a relative term, whereas *impossible* is absolute and would allow no possibility of improvement.

Each chapter includes a Reflective Recess for your deliberation about issues presented in the chapter. Chapter 1 discusses schools and the people in them as mosaic, tapestry, and web. The public character of the school and changing characteristics of school constituents are addressed through the contradiction of constancy and change. Traditional assumptions about the structure, process and content, people, and context of schools are shown to continue behind the facades of change programs, which are merely variations on themes.

Chapter 2 focuses on women in schools and on "being" and "becoming" in the increasingly diverse environment of schools. The significance of women as resources is contrasted with the number of women represented in school administration. Women's socialization, formal and informal barriers, women and leadership, motivation and mission, and priorities and practices are addressed with respect to gender as a cultural phenomenon.

Chapter 3 explores issues in creating empowering cultures in schools, for which the female perspective can be instrumental—

considering adult growth, development, and learning. The issues of power and powerlessness, networks and relationships, and patterns of communication are discussed as they relate to the significance of bringing people into a variety of roles in an effort to challenge the environment of work.

The concluding Chapter 4 focuses on leadership and learning communities. An examination of effective leadership is presented, with defining qualities exemplified by women educators. The significance of modeling, mentoring, vision, and reflection are discussed as they relate to leadership as teaching and learning. An annotated bibliography follows Chapter 4 and contains works that more fully address the issues presented in this book.

Schools and the People in Them

People is all everything is, all it has ever been, all it can ever be.

(WILLIAM SAROYAN)

Schools, because of the people in them, are at the same time mosaic, tapestry, and web. Schools are human enterprises, nothing more and nothing less, and therefore the relationships in them are complex. The profound meaning in this statement is often overlooked as a result of our preoccupations with the peripheral tasks of administering schools. We speak of schools as if they were inanimate.

The public character of the school and the characteristics of school constituents have changed dramatically over the last several years. It seems that this should have significant implications for how and why we conduct schools as we do. However, we have only modestly addressed and tentatively embraced these issues. If we envision making schools more meaningful, and more successful for those who live and work in them, reshaping the world of schools means attending to how human diversity influences the culture of schools.

Simply put, diversity refers to difference and variety. Form a mental picture about a state, New Mexico for instance. What comes to mind? What does the geography look like? What are the characteristics of the people who live there? The land in New Mexico is diverse—different and varied. It has deserts, and it has mountains that exceed 12,000 feet in altitude. The characteristics of the people who live there are equally as diverse—different and varied. Likewise, when we form a mental picture of people in schools, we should use discretion lest they disappear behind our personal definitions of them.

This chapter explores constancy and change in schools. The contradiction is addressed in terms of facades and variations on themes that accompany the re's—restructuring, reform, renewal, reculturing—and associated change initiatives.

Schools: Constancy and Change

Anyone who has spent any time in schools is likely aware of changes in student populations. Consider the shifts and projections in the demographic nature of school populations throughout the nation. In 1976, 24% of the school enrollment was non-white; in 1984, almost 30% of school enrollment was non-white; by the year 2020, it is projected that 46% of students will be non-white (Cushner, McClelland, & Safford, 1992). Although these percentages might be much higher in certain districts, states, or geographic regions, the potential impact is not exclusive.

Many schools and school districts might not mirror the ethnic and racial diversity of the nation at large but, in all probability, do reflect altered family structures. Over 60% of our students live in families where both parents, or the only parent, work outside the home. By 1995, this percentage is expected to rise to 75% (Cushner, McClelland, & Stafford, 1992). We are made acutely aware that children who live in single-parent homes have become the norm rather than the exception. These, and countless other social circumstances, have had and will continue to have a significant influence on schools. It is rare, however, that these circumstances prompt changes in the deep structure and organization of schools.

The time frame of the school day and the school year are examples of deep structure, organization, and tradition. For example, there are very few schools that accommodate adult workdays by beginning later and ending later. Nor have schools accommodated to those who are single parents, many of whom are educators. Having said that, I can hear voices that proclaim why it cannot be done differently in a particular school or district!

Schools are not isolated from the conditions of society at large, and although the legal ramifications of *in loco parentis* may have diminished somewhat over the years, our moral obligations have been magnified. This does not imply that schools can, or should, be held responsible for single-handedly addressing the multitude of issues and public problems generated from private lives. It does imply that we have a moral responsibility to do our utmost to minimize the negative effects of these circumstances on those who are received in schools!

If we consider issues that affect children, we would find considerable similarity as they apply to adults in schools. People in schools have other dimensions to their lives. They have characteristics of identification and a life history. It is not unusual to find faculty and staff members who represent the milieu of social circumstance—they are members of minorities, they are single parents, and so on. The diverse nature of schools is manifested in ways beyond what is immediately observable. *Gender* as a cultural phenomenon, a way of being, thinking, and doing, is an example.

Schools are complex organizations in purpose, function, and form. The models and prescriptions for reforming schools have not addressed issues of fundamental change—they are derived still from perspectives of bureaucratic rationality. Although, to some degree, order and predictability are necessary for organizations to function, schools are not ordinary, rational organizations. Typically, adhering to bureaucratic rationality precludes alternatives to the status quo by fixating on legitimation in lines of authority, regulation, and control of social reality (Rizvi, 1987).

The context of schools as being representative of the people in them is questionable. For example, the majority of policymakers and members of the administrative hierarchy continues to be dominated by males to the degree that schools have been referred to as "educational harems." The major reform reports of the last decade acknowledge the need to address our diverse culture, particularly issues of ethnicity, race, and exceptionality. We must presume that gender is to be inferred.

The reality of working in patriarchal-bureaucratic institutions and our vision of what schools could be, should be, or ought to be clash power against critical consciousness. Changing the way we think about schools, and who leads them, means challenging many of the givens. Addressing the competing functions of schools, preserving society *and* changing it, requires alternative perspectives and approaches. The rationale for any particular approach is based on how preserving schools and changing them are defined and by whom. Often, persistent problems in schools are seen as if they were new. Most problems and issues are not new, however, but are, essentially, recurrences of their historical antecedents and the inefficacy of remedial efforts. As Sarason (1990) put it,

> Like almost all other complex traditional social organizations, the schools will accommodate in ways that require little or no change. This is not to say that the accommodation is insincere or deliberately cosmetic but rather that the strength of the status quo . . . almost automatically rules out options for change in that status quo. (p. 35)

The domain of our understanding of and attention to curriculum issues, administrative structure, allocation of resources, power relationships, decision making, assessment, and standards must be widened to include multiple perspectives. Change in policy does not necessarily result in positive or effective changes in practice. We must think differently about human capacity.

If we were to accept the notion that schools as social institutions could become learning communities, life in schools would be characterized by engaging those who have been marginalized and by applauding diversity. Barth (1990) describes a good school as one that respects differences, a place where differences are looked for, attended to, and celebrated as opportunities for learning. Further, he suggests that differences in philosophy, style, and passion are remarkable sources of ideas for improvement and that what is important is not sameness but diversity. Is this troubling and uncomfortable for some of us? Most certainly it is.

Very few educators have had the opportunity to design and develop a new school in its entirety. If posed with that challenge, chances are that many of us would find parts of what we created somewhat like the dragon that we are attempting to slay. If *you* were to design and develop a school, how would the notion of mosaic, tapestry, and web be considered with respect to constancy and change? The Reflective Recess in Figure 1.1 poses questions for your deliberation.

Reflective Recess

You are going to design and develop a school. Take a few minutes to reflect on the location of the school, the students, and the community your school will serve. With these in mind, consider the following questions:

1. Who would you involve in the planning?
2. What do you value in those you would select?
3. How would you go about initiating and continuing the planning process?
4. What is your vision about what the school would look like?
5. What is your vision of plans and designs for the following?
   a. The organization of the school day, week, year
   b. Curriculum and instruction for students
   c. Roles and relationships of adults
   d. Professional development
   e. Community involvement
   f. Assessment and evaluation
   g. Programs and provisions for student associations

Figure 1.1. Reflective Recess: A New School or a New School Order?

Did you find yourself puzzled by the magnitude of the challenge? How often did you find yourself thinking about some ideal and regressing with thoughts about why it could not be accomplished? Was your thinking limited by your own personal views about schools? What did you envision as the potential contributions of others? What were your governing assumptions about the structure of schools, educational processes, people, and context? Looking in retrospect, what was traditional and what was not? Why?

Thinking about schools differently is difficult, but it is less difficult than inventing them. The commitment to imagine what could be must go beyond creating facades and ineffective variations on old bureaucratic themes to become viable variations on themes that encourage success for adults and children in schools.

Facades and Variations on Themes

Expectations about what school should be like and look like come from our own history and personal experience in schools. We remember those times that were pleasant and those that were unpleasant. We remember those people who touched our lives in positive ways and, perhaps, those whose influence was negative. When we are asked to think about people who influenced our lives, rarely do we find a list that does not include a teacher.

Parents and other members of the community come to our schools accompanied by their own baggage of memory. They view with suspicion what is new or different, regardless of its educational worth or merit. It is amazing how often we are unable to provide substantive replies when we are asked to justify or explain why we do what we do. There are a few reasons but more frequent excuses. Unfortunately, in schools today more emphasis is placed on what works than on what matters.

Many of our initiatives to reform, restructure, reculture, or renew schools seem to be facades. They vary little from traditional assumptions about the structure, process and content, people, and context of schools. Some, however few, variations from these assumptions are based on ideas larger than the individual, the classroom, the school, or the community. Consider these prevailing assumptions and traditions that trap us in a narrow set of parameters based on what has been rather than what could be.

1. The Structure of the School. The structure of the school is derived from the notion of bureaucratic rationality and hierarchy as the most appropriate organizational pattern for establishing uniformity, accountability, authority, and power and for assessing achievement and standards of performance. We perpetuate the regulatory orientation of school improvement focused on achieving policy goals. This is reinforced by a line of associated assumptions—leadership and management focused on control and coordination; design and conduct of work based on uniformity; and decision making and accountability derived from inconsonant sources.

School-based decision making and school-based management are examples of attempts to alter the control structure of school. In many instances, efforts to decentralize decision making, authority, and responsibility have *added* layers in the hierarchy, and the units of governance have not been representative at all. Mandates are often so prescriptive that schools with genuine involvement of faculty, staff, and community have had their domains of decisions and bases of support limited. This seems to do little toward acknowledging the unique aspects of schools and the people in them. Unfortunately, the dominant structures remain intact and continue to constrain attempts to develop teams, family plans, and non-grade-specific instruction.

2. The Process and Content of the School. Process and content in schools are based on ideas about how teaching and learning occur. The ways students and teachers, school days and years, and the curriculum are organized are related to dominant assumptions about teaching and learning. With all too few exceptions, patterns reveal age or grade grouping, tracking or ability grouping, and discrete or segmented curriculum and instructional delivery.

Curricular and instructional change usually involve only superficial modifications of what is currently present. Often, developing alternative perspectives about pedagogy is confined through control systems or assessment programs. A number of change initiatives establish strategies for comparing the educational outcomes of schools, districts, and states. This results in competition becoming the incentive for organizational and individual performance,

with precise consequences for failure, and further deters considering options based on specific community context and student
needs.

3. *Assumptions About People in Schools.* Assumptions about the people in schools stem from beliefs about human nature in general.
Efforts to change schools continue to be predicated on the notion
that people must be coerced, externally directed, and monitored
regularly in order to improve. Although these tenets may hold true
for some, they imprison others and deny any effort to create environments based on collaboration rather than on competition and
compliance.

The extent to which roles and relationships in schools have been
altered has been more limited by human *un*imagination and inflex-
ibility than by fiscal restraints. Differentiating assignments, expanding or reducing non-instructional-related assignments for teachers,
and increasing parent and community involvement have been the
least expensive and most effective of change efforts. However, involvement in decision making continues to leave some constituent
groups marginalized.

4. *The Context of School.* The context of school continues to serve as
a sorting mechanism for the social, economic, ethnic, racial, and
gender characteristics of the larger society. Further, what has been
asked of schools in dealing with social issues such as poverty,
housing, health, and crime has been seen by them as the addition
of one more load to an already full cart. If school is a community
within a larger community, what better way to contradict this notion of social issues as too much than through the integration of
services in school and society. Too many schools, as well as service
agencies, remain foreign, foreboding, and uninviting places for too
many constituents.

The facades and variations on themes for changing schools are
many. However, real change in schools cannot take place without
fundamental change in the leadership and culture of schools that
reflects the unique contributions of all members. The commitment
to bureaucracy as the most credible form of organization remains
a basic belief in most schools and school systems. As if too basic to

be challenged, acceptance of differential roles and status, clearly divided responsibility and authority, and rules governing relationships and interactions remains. This becomes the social order of the school and the school culture, and people become important only as they fit into those structures. Meaning is lost, and people are stripped of their individual talent and ability to contribute.

I remain convinced that all children are, at the same time, gifted and at-risk. Perhaps communities and adults in schools are as well. This will continue if we do not become more sensitive and pliable in our efforts to utilize our human resources wisely.

Conclusion

There is an array of very different streams of thought about preserving schools and changing them and about teaching, learning, and leading. Setting lofty goals for schools to become flawless or perfect institutions denies the human frailty inherent in an enterprise of people. Yet, schools and the people in them can be more successful and productive and achieve higher levels of accomplishment through extending the parameters of how we view structure, process and content, people, and context in schools. Viewing people in schools as mosaic, tapestry, and web prompts us to think about better ways of utilizing human resources for being and becoming in a diverse environment.

Women in Schools: Being and Becoming in a Diverse Environment

Among human beings . . . there is clear evidence that although individual men may love individual women with great depth and devotion, the male world as a whole does not.

(JESSIE BERNARD, *The Female World*)

Women are a significant resource for learning how to lead schools. Although studies of women and school leadership continue to be limited in comparison to studies of men, a great deal of information exists about women and the world of schools. Women have influenced and made notable contributions throughout the history of education, yet—although women continue to represent the majority of teachers—the representation of women in school administration continues to be disproportional. The career paths, personal characteristics, and motivational orientations of women who have broken through the "glass ceiling" of school administration are largely different from those of men. Accordingly, these variables have profound implications for leading and changing schools.

This chapter extends the discussion about schools and the value of the people in them begun in Chapter 1 by examining women's representation in positions of leadership. What we have learned about women's socialization, formal and informal barriers to women's advancement, women's motivation and mission, and women's priorities and practice are discussed relative to myths about women and leadership.

The Numbers and Nature of Women's Representation

Some would suggest that the gates to positions in educational leadership have been flung wide open for women, yet the existing evidence does not support this claim. A 1992 publication by the American Association of School Administrators, *Women and Minorities in School Administration: Facts and Figures 1989-1990*, strengthens the point that Shakeshaft (1987) makes regarding the underrepresentation of women in educational administration. Although the facts and figures reveal modest representation of women and minorities in the superintendency (Figure 2.1), assistant superintendency (Figure 2.2), and principalship (Figure 2.3), the numbers of minority women in these positions reflect an even greater disparity.

Three propositions attempt to explain why women are underrepresented in administration—women's socialization, formal and informal barriers to women, and myths about women's leadership.

Women's Socialization

Inherent in socialization theories about women in education are assumptions that women are unsuited for administrative work and that teaching is a distinctly separate career from administration rather than an extension of it (Ortiz & Marshall, 1988). The gender-role stereotypes that pervade our culture continue to produce people who function within the parameters of their socialization, which is more often than not restrictive and narrow. The

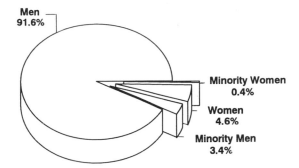

Figure 2.1. Representation in the Superintendency

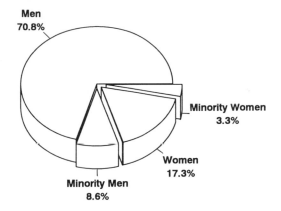

Figure 2.2. Representation in the Assistant Superintendency

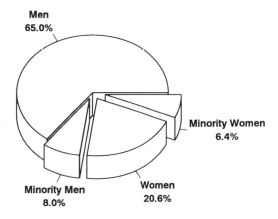

Figure 2.3. Representation in the Principalship

environment of schools mirrors this socialization when the concept of "one's place" is embraced. This inhibits all people, and particularly women, from recognizing their personal capacity to lead.

A number of scenarios exhibit these stereotypes about gender and socialization. Think for a moment about the range of opinions regarding gender and boardrooms, budgets, bargaining, and busses. What are the expectations regarding who makes the coffee or takes minutes? Whose expectations? What are the beliefs about who can best make decisions about purchasing mechanical equipment? Whose beliefs? What are the prevailing assumptions about negotiating and collective bargaining? Whose assumptions? What are the speculations about gender and interest in, knowledge of, and the ability to make decisions about bias-ply versus steel-belted radial tires? Whose speculations?

Many women are capable of performing in all these roles and of rendering quality decisions in all theses areas. Such capacity is not, necessarily, solely a function of biological description. Stereotyping and bias about women's backgrounds, experiences, and interests have produced unfavorable attitudes about women's ability to function in certain situations and in particular positions.

I recall discussing my interest in automobile restoration with a faculty colleague. He told me about a car club to which he belonged and invited me to attend one evening. As a postscript, however, he indicated that the women who attended brought things to do, such as board games or cards, while the men talked cars. Whether meant in jest or seriousness, the meaning in the message was clear. Informal barriers often become formalized.

Formal and Informal Barriers

Barriers to women's advancement are informal as well as formal. Formal barriers, such as preparation and certification, may not be as imposing as the informal ones, such as inclusion and association with the center of power in organizations. Without doubt, the representation of women in educational administration preparation programs has increased dramatically over the last few years. However, the contention that there are few qualified female candidates lingers as a barrier.

Lack of formal and informal networks hampers women's efforts in gaining access to positions in administrative ranks—and certain positions in particular. The evidence about women's representation would be even more compelling if we were to slice the pies in Figures 2.1, 2.2, and 2.3 to illustrate the percentages of women in urban, suburban, and rural superintendencies, by type of assistant superintendencies, and as elementary, middle, and high school principals. Women superintendents are more often found in small districts, women assistant superintendents are more often in staff specialist or supervisory positions, and women principals are more often found at the elementary school level. The perception that women are not tough enough to handle the political environment or the discipline problems of a high school remains strong.

The elementary principalship, as well as certain central office positions, has been considered by some to be a dead-end post. Given that more women occupy these kinds of positions, this view becomes a barrier and intensifies the degree of women's exclusion. One of the reasons for this contention may be that these positions are not as publicly visible as the superintendency or a high school principalship. Existing myths about women and leadership are sustained because of formal and informal barriers.

Myths About Women and Leadership

Myths about women's leadership continue to be critical aspects in the selection of school administrators. Although there has been a growing preference for approaches and behaviors in school leadership typically associated with a female leadership perspective, these preferences are not held as strongly as are the convictions about what a principal or superintendent should look like or act like. In many instances, there is more in common ideologically between women and men than among women or among men. The issue then becomes one of the politics of gender and the degree that women find legitimation in their ability to function in a dominant patriarchal organization.

Politics of gender are also evident in the perception of men as elementary teachers or administrators, although there is quite a demand for men as elementary teachers, particularly men who are members of racial minorities. This has more to do with matters of having appropriate role models than matters of competence or ability. We might question why there is not equal emphasis in seeking women to fill positions that have traditionally been linked to men.

The literature documents little or no difference in the competence or ability of men and women in administration. However, criteria used in examining competence or ability were generated from what we have learned about the administrative behavior of men (predominately white men). Other findings document the markedly different ways in which men and women administer schools. As Shakeshaft (1987) points out, describing male and female leadership behavior as "equally effective" is not synonymous with "identical to."

Beyond management and administration, leadership in schools involves considering what is known about teaching and learning. We have learned much about expert teaching and learning in the last quarter century. Despite this, a chasm exists between the boardroom and the classroom. It has been said that "women teach and men lead." This has held true since the beginning of the common school. The way women and men are viewed and the way roles are negotiated often replicate the labor and power structure outside of schools. This is seen in high-profile or charismatic actions that have little to do with what schools are really all about. Aggressiveness and action alone are not the only fundamental aspects in creating schools as communities of learners. Thought must accompany action and critical thought must accompany meaningful action.

One perspective of leadership can be summarized by stating that to lead implies that there must be those who will follow. Another perspective holds that leadership involves facilitating and enabling others to make contributions while making our own contributions. Leading and learning are collective and collaborative efforts in schools as communities. Sergiovanni (1991) discusses building a "shared covenant" as a fundamental aspect of moral leadership. Glickman (1990) has us think about a "cause beyond oneself." These propositions prompt us to think about our leadership as facilitating the growth and development of others while enlarging our own capacity to lead. Transforming the goals and aspirations of organizational members is a characteristic motivational orientation and mission of women's leadership.

Motivation and Mission

Shakeshaft (1987) points out that aggregate profiles of women in school leadership reveal dissimilarities in career profiles from those of men in administration. Several models exist to explain the complex processes of career decision making, and defining the concept of *career* for men and women in similar terms can be disputed (Biklen, 1985).

Ascendancy for men in educational organizations has typically been a move-up or move-out orientation, whereas the teaching profession has been responsive to women moving in and out as life circumstances warranted. Women's paths into administration are often unplanned and serendipitous. Women appear to have a commitment to teaching at a very early age, unlike the commitment of men to teaching as a secondary career option (Shakeshaft, 1987). Many women in school administration attribute the respect that they received as teacher as an important element in why they were selected as an administrator.

I have found that even though there have been more women than men in my graduate educational administration classes, most of the women express little or no desire to become an administrator. When an interest is communicated, it is rarely toward becoming a superintendent or a principal. When questioned about this reticence, their responses reveal negative perceptions of the positions vis-à-vis poor role models. Those few who do aspire to become superintendents or principals see it as a way for them to make significant changes in school life. Others indicate a clear preference for positions that do not distance them from teaching or the classroom. The motivations and missions of women who aspire to positions in administration appear to be inextricably tied to improving their own and others' lives. This is evident in the what we have learned about women's priorities and women's practice.

Priorities and Practice

We can all recall conversations where an experience is being discussed and others interject impressions about the same experience that are greatly different from our own. Although we all might have been involved in the same experience, this does not mean that we experienced it similarly. So it is with women's experience in the world of schools. The fundamental tasks of administering schools have no gender identification, yet what has emphasis in priority and practice may. Primary to women's work in schools is a focus on relationships, teaching and learning, and establishing a sense of community. Gilligan (1982) discusses women's concern about relationships as an "ethic of care." This is evident in women administrators' frequent interaction with others, in the kinds and amount of information that is shared, and in the time spent communicating with multiple constituents (Shakeshaft, 1987).

That women enter education with a primary commitment to teaching is manifested in the climate and culture of schools that women administer. There appears to be greater emphasis on leadership for learning and actions directed toward achievement. The management metaphor for schools is contrary to female organizational culture. However, there are exceptions in how this is played out in practice in the dominant culture of schools.

As many studies have shown, there is an integration of male and female characteristics in effective leaders. Lightfoot's (1983) work points to male leaders who consciously sought to feminize their style with respect to relationships and interaction, trust and collegiality, and shared responsibility and authority. The public self and private self of the woman administrator are often interconnected. The connection between an individual's life inside and outside of school influences behavior, attitudes, and the level of commitment and energy that is directed to one or the other. With this statement in mind, look at the questions in the Reflective Recess in Figure 2.4.

Were the statements in the first item disconcerting to you? Why? What do you see as the connection between the first and second questions regarding living and working in a diverse environment, women and leadership, and adult growth, development, and learning in schools?

Reflective Recess

1. Consider the following statements and their implications for
being and becoming in schools:
   a. I grew tired of my teaching position and wanted a new
   challenge. I needed a change.
   b. I'd like to be a superintendent, but there aren't many
   women in the superintendency. There are a few female
   assistant superintendents, but men seem to become the
   superintendents.
   c. I'm not looking for a principal's job. I enjoy not being at
   the top and having to deal with the pressures of administrators and accommodating to the school board and other
   groups.
2. What do you see or believe exists in your school, district, or
community about the following?
   a. Formal and informal barriers
   b. Motivation and mission
   c. Priorities and practice

Figure 2.4. Reflective Recess: Women in Schools

Conclusion

Stereotypes and assumptions about race, ethnicity, and gender
have produced an educational climate that fails to foster the emotional, intellectual, and professional development of all people in
schools. We have seen from the example of women in schools how
this is manifest, but we have also seen how women can be instrumental to the necessary changes. How we perceive cultural attributes
plays a large part in the experiences that we provide for others and
the degree that others are viewed as significant players in the organization. Our expectations of others become critical factors in
how their success or failure is measured. How we behave and respond to others' capacity and aspirations is influenced by the beliefs and assumptions we hold about difference and diversity.

The Female Perspective: Creating Empowering Cultures

Nothing will ever be attempted if all possible objections must first be overcome.

(SAMUEL JOHNSON)

If we want to develop schools as empowering cultures, we have to understand the growth and development of people in the school organization. Group growth results from individual growth, and just as individuals have particular stages of development, so do organizations. This chapter begins with a discussion of adult growth, development, and learning in schools. The implications for creating a culture that is empowering are addressed through challenging the school environment of work. Power and powerlessness, developing networks and relationships, and patterns of communication are critical dimensions explored here.

Adults in Schools: Growth, Development, and Learning

The notion of schools as communities of learners must take into consideration the nature of adults in schools. Beyond the difference of physical attributes, adults have distinctly differing philosophies about learning and life—and our behaviors and attitudes are formed from the assumptions and beliefs that we hold. Imagine the contrast in life experiences that we would find between a 22-year-old teacher and a 65-year-old teacher. This does not necessarily imply that the veteran would be the mentor and the novice the protégé. There is great potential for reciprocity in teaching and learning. The degree to which this breadth and depth of personal and professional experience is utilized in schools depends on norms of collegiality and collaboration.

Collegiality and collaboration require an awareness and appreciation for inherent human difference. Imagine the range of preferences you might find in people's profiles on the Myers-Briggs Type Inventory. Most likely, some would have preferences similar to your own, particularly if you were responsible for their recruitment and selection. We tend to place greater merit on those who are relatively like-minded. Any disharmony that exists may illustrate differences in introversion and extroversion, intuition and sensing, thinking and feeling, and judging and perceiving. However discomforting these differences may be, they can also be endowments to the organization if utilized appropriately.

A fundamental premise of schools is that they should be organized and function around the developmental needs of children. However, attention to the needs of the adults in schools is crucial. Consider what we have learned about adult development and learning applied to career cycles and the implications of this for schools.

Early research on adult development suggests that people move through predictable life stages or phases. Later research suggests that adult development is less age- or stage-related and more based on responses to crises or life events. Erikson (1968) discussed adult development from the perspectives of *intimacy versus isolation, generativity versus self-absorption,* and *integrity versus despair.*

Adults in schools have little meaningful contact with each other; changing this fact would enhance adult development. Creating conditions for sharing expertise and sharing leadership can be helpful in resolving concerns of intimacy and of isolation. The conflict between generativity and self-absorption arises from the lack of balance between nurturing others' growth and development and being nurtured. Organizational norms that increase professional integrity rather than norms that result in despair can have profound consequences.

For the most part, there is little difference in the responsibilities and rewards of novice or veteran practitioners. The school hierarchy prevents opportunities for many to gain access to positions and to function in roles of advanced status that tap their experience, knowledge, and skills.

The interplay between social and psychological factors is a complex issue in adulthood. Schools must reflect work settings that are responsive to adult developmental needs. Separating personal and professional life is difficult—and for women, almost impossible. Phase theories help to identify issues and life tasks in adult growth and development. Providing appropriate opportunities for personal and professional growth must be given adequate attention if we are to make a positive impact on organizational growth.

Kohlberg's (1984) work focuses on adults' stages of moral reasoning and response to authority, evaluation, decision making, and collaboration. The connection between how we think and how we act and the way we deal with problems and dilemmas in school are partially determined by our degree of development in moral reasoning. Loevinger (1976) explains the relationship of ego development and change resistance. She cautions about making broad-brush assumptions about the abilities of adults to be introspective, reflective, and self-directed.

I have been somewhat dismayed when reviewing course syllabi that are based on my convictions that adult graduate students are introspective, reflective, and self-directed learners. Although increasingly less so, it seemed that the essence was "tell me what you want, how you want it done, and when." This prompted me to introspect and reflect on my own experiences in school in order to understand their expectations. Quite simply, from kindergarten through graduate school, many of us are taught and led by being told what, where, when, how, and occasionally why. I hold strongly to my convictions that learning can be facilitated through introspective, reflective, and self-directed activities. However, this is not an expectation but a goal.

Although we might hope that educators enter the workplace properly prepared and with exemplary skills, this is a bit naive. Becoming self-directed is a goal to be achieved rather than an inherent attribute in most of us. A number of variables contribute to one's ability to introspect, reflect, and become self-directed. Our life history, developmental stage or phase, motivational orientation, and socialization have great bearing on these capacities. Group growth results from individual growth. Ultimately, growth must begin with the individual, with the self, before we can extend our expectations for others—or the organization—to change. There are as many teachable moments for adults in schools as there are for children.

The difference in men's and women's development emphasizes the significance of bringing men and women into a variety of educational roles. Encouraging men to be in direct contact with children and placing women in leadership roles expands experiences and affords children the opportunity to see people in multiple roles. Efforts such as these encourage building cultures of enrichment and growth rather than cultures of confinement.

Schools have periods of birth and early growth, a midlife, and maturity. According to Schein (1985), an understanding of what an organization's culture is and what it is doing for constituents, regardless of how it came to be, is often missing. The elements of culture may be retained, strengthened, or refined depending on the degree of *flexibility* rather than *strength* of the culture. At certain points in our history, the factory-model school was representative of a larger environment that was less messy and complex. This environment no longer exists, and schools are not insulated from outside forces. Although schools have similar origins and functions, the internal and external environments are often quite different. Organizations function as a result of the actions of individuals and groups based on value orientations and basic assumptions.

Challenging the Environment of Work

It seems to me that much of the ammunition that has been fired at schools has produced a rather dispersed pattern on the target. Moreover, the target has been somewhat ill-defined. Goodlad's (1983) comment about the school as the unit of change seems to be a most viable approach to getting a tighter pattern on the target. Put another way, work in schools must be viewed differently if we expect to facilitate change in an increasingly diverse environment.

The reward structure in schools is upside down and front-loaded. For example, a teacher's first year in the profession differs little from the last year. Being removed from the classroom into the principal's office, or from the principal's office to the central office, is the common reward for accomplishment or longevity. The voices of those in schools resound with messages of disempowerment and frustration. Paths to growth and advancement are unclear and hierarchical rather than latitudinal. The focus of attention is on dependence and the way things are rather than on the way they might be. Increasing the degree of collaboration and norms of collegiality among adults in schools is the primary challenge of creating productive work environments. The relationship between principals and teachers is *sine qua non*. Because schools are human enterprises, many of the dilemmas that confront us are consequences of power and powerlessness.

Power and Powerlessness

Burbules (1986) provides us with a way to look at power in organizations as relational and necessary. The circumstances that bring people together may reveal conflicting or compatible backgrounds, interests, presumptions, and expectations of certain roles or positions that enhance or delimit what are seen as possibilities. Further, personal traits predispose some people to carrying out dominant or submissive roles in relationships.

Powerlessness limits our confidence, our ability to perform, and our sense of well-being. The hierarchical organization of schools tends to perpetuate the status quo of how roles are defined and how possibilities and personal endeavors are determined, enhanced, or limited. Using power as a means to coerce, manipulate, and gain compliance increases our sense of oppression and constrains us from exploring options and alternatives. Power relationships are as real in the way schools function and are organized as they are in the larger society. We see this illustrated in the hierarchy of roles, certain instructional practices, school and classroom organization, and in curriculum design and content. In the larger community, it is reflected in power relationships based on class, gender, race, and ethnicity.

Power and powerlessness are pivotal aspects of the culture of schools. The concept of power has both covert and overt aspects and the manner through which conflict is resolved and collaboration is achieved depends on power relationships. Women's early socialization and the exclusion of women from networks of information and opportunity contribute to the discrepancy in comparing power between men and women. Further, the male culture often views power as zero-sum, whereas the female culture views power as limitless (Shaef, 1985). The most vital lesson from research on power and influence is that the more people believe that they can influence the organization, the more effective and productive the organization will be.

Differences in the way men and women exercise power and authority may be a result of early socialization, when men are encouraged to be competitive and aggressive and women are not. Women's assertive styles are still often interpreted as being overly aggressive. Bias in expectations and perceptions tends to influence the behavior of the powerless, which knows no gender. Women and minorities tend to be socially isolated and confronted with unique standards. Subsequently, these are passed along to children and affect their behavior, aspirations, and perceptions of others. To be effective in counteracting self-fulfilling prophecies, credit for our success must be given to competence rather than luck. Moreover, we must learn to acknowledge our own and others' contributions and to take informed risks.

Indicators of powerlessness include losing sight of the bigger picture, short-term focus, an inability to delegate, control of information, resistance to change, use of indirect methods of influence, and seeking homogeneity rather than diversity. Empowering cultures, however, promote continual examination of policies and procedures, reward intelligent risk, have a clear connection between what individuals do and the organization's success, and have norms of trust. Removing the barriers that make it difficult for individuals to assume responsibility for their own and the organization's success is essential in creating an empowering organization. Likewise, individuals must choose to accept responsibility for their own behavior and realize the impact on organizational success. Developing networks and relationships predicated on trust is essential.

Developing Networks and Relationships

Patterns of mistrust and pessimism must be discarded if we are to develop relationships that foster creativity and initiative. The characteristics that positively affect others' lives and contribute to success involve mutual trust, reciprocal influence, synergy, respect for diverse backgrounds and expertise, and commitment. Self-interest and mistrust are as much matters of intensity and degree as are relationships founded in "the good of the order" and trust. Differences in hierarchical positions, power, and authority do not have to be the only determining factor in the quality of relationships—each member possesses knowledge, skills, and expertise.

Crossing the formal boundaries of control and accountability is essential to interdependence and collective effort. Although certain roles and positions are accompanied by some scope of authority and accountability, there is also greater responsibility. The chasm that exists between the "them" and the "us" results from lack of understanding, inappropriate or faulty communication, and lack of commitment to common goals. Diminishing the conditions that promote self-interest rather than a common vision is critical. Notice how often members of an organization use *we* instead of *I, my,* or *me.* Successes and failures must be seen as mutual concerns.

As mentioned previously, relationships are a fundamental aspect of the female culture. The quality of interactions depends largely on the degree of trust that exists, the degree that creativity and risk taking are encouraged, and the focus of commitment. Even though we may realize that disagreement and conflict are inevitable, our leadership behavior needs to be based on creating supportive relationships and human connections. Whatever organizational and individual achievements and successes occur do so because of relationships between people rather than because of programs or fulfilling particular job descriptions.

Much of what does not get accomplished can be attributed to a prevailing tone of fear—faculty and staff may fear principals, principals may fear superintendents, superintendents may fear school boards, school boards may fear constituents, and so on. To the extent that this fear exists, it serves only to perpetuate the vicious cycle of mistrust and to invite self-interest and detachment. Indicators of the presence of fear are districts where schools and communities have become adversaries and systems where those in positions of leadership have created the "good old boy" or the "good old girl" syndrome.

Dealing with fear and mistrust, developing networks and relationships, and creating empowering cultures can be an excruciatingly slow process, messy, and fraught with dilemmas. Efforts toward creating an empowering culture can provide a higher level of organizational sophistication and maturity through gaining new understandings and challenging practice that limits possibilities. Whatever the extent of our political astuteness, it is complemented only by our ingenuity. As educators, we have taken more than our fair share of criticisms—many of the criticisms have merit, but others are the bitter harvest of our reliance on outdated beliefs, customs, and habits. Diversity in schools and society demands that we challenge our ways of operating.

The gap between our ability to envision and to act on that vision seems great when we confront our own and others' values, assumptions, and beliefs. If we want to facilitate change in the diverse environment of schools, we must begin by getting a clear picture of the desired change and then engage others in a collective effort to bring it about. Rather than thinking about casting away what is there, we need to think about what arrangements exist and how we can work within those to improve them.

Fullan (1992) offers us a way to look at the myths and truths associated with change and failed efforts and proposes some orientations for thinking about change. These orientations are not isolated but are to be understood in aggregate. Here are six of them:

(1) Our maps of change often do not accurately represent the territory we have to cross; (2) solutions to problems and dilemmas are not easy and are often unknown; (3) symbols take precedence over substance; (4) superficial solutions are often structural rather than cultural; (5) natural responses to transitions are not necessarily resistance; and (6) significant changes are often tightly linked to individuals or groups and do not become institutionalized.

Facilitating change requires thinking and reflecting on the viable human connections that are involved. Putting the ownership of change in perspective involves learning new things while deriving personal meaning. We have adequate information at our disposal about levels of concern and change. As facilitators of change, it is important that we realize that opposition to change is not necessarily predicated on ignorance or apathy. Our approaches must be grounded in setting up conditions for success through taking informed risks and accepting uncertainty. Whatever the degree of acceptance or rejection, learning can occur.

The sentiments that accompany any effort to change are based on certain beliefs or convictions; knowing whether our own and others' opinions and attitudes are superficial beliefs or deeply held convictions is very important. Both have a source of origination, both are somehow maintained over time, and both have some degree of evolution. It would seem that convictions are beliefs that become stable over time, are attached to strong feelings, and are accompanied by depth of knowledge. In other words, a belief becomes a conviction through information, intensity, and commitment. Note well, however, that simply explaining an idea does not plant the seeds of beliefs that become the garden of conviction.

Many prescriptions for changing today's schools tend to focus on seeking solutions that are timeless rather than ways to continuously shape and reshape the schools. Likely, our efforts and energies would be wiser spent on exploring ways to deal with the perpetual problems and daily dilemmas in schools more successfully. There are rich and untapped human resources in our schools. Turf protection and shelter from criticism must give way to encouraging participation, developing group identity, and facilitating inclusion. This means changing our habitual ways of communicating and interacting with one another.

Establishing Patterns of Communication

The patterns of communication in organizations vary as much as the organizations themselves. Communication is patterned culturally and is interpretive, formal, and informal. If organizational and institutional structures are created by communication, then communication is influenced by those structures. It seems to make little difference whether an organization is large or small, rural or urban, the formal communication flow is typically hierarchical. Informal communication is lateral, vertical, unrestricted, and unendorsed. When we really think about it, informal communication is by far the most potent. This is where interpretation of formal communication occurs and how meaning is derived for organizational members.

The communicative behavior of individuals in groups varies with the demands of the situation and the characteristics of group members. Whether because of race, ethnicity, gender, or other attributes, people have particular emotional responses, knowledge, and cultural frameworks that come into play when interacting with others. Certain concepts can provide us with the intellectual tools needed for understanding and addressing human interaction in diverse settings. Emotional experiences resulting from encounters with cultural difference include anxiety, disconfirmed expectations, ambiguity, and confronting prejudice.

When unfamiliar demands are placed on individuals or groups, typical affective responses are anxiety and apprehension. Even though people are essentially social beings, schools have tended to be places where people operate in isolation. The level of personal and professional maturity is a significant factor in thought processes and in how events are interpreted. Cultural phenomena and socialization are also critical. Many people find certain aspects of cultural knowledge difficult to understand, such as the task and social balance of groups, locus of control, approaches to decision making, and attitudes about creativity. Other aspects that may be problematic include the dimensions of time and space, language, roles, group versus individual importance, rituals, and values.

The ways that men and women communicate in mixed gender groups vary with the demands of the situation as well as individ-

ual characteristics. In collaborative groups, women tend to partic-
ipate more readily than in groups that are hierarchically bound.
For the most part, the comments that men make are given more
outward attention, and many women are silenced. Although this
has little to do with the relative independence, assertiveness, and
self-confidence of many women, it supports the traditional and instrumental role of gender in society.

People in schools are often isolated from sources that can provide information and ideas. We become myopic and lack creativity.
Resolving important issues in schools demands bringing people
together so that human capacities enrich decisions and life in
schools. Unfortunately, the structure in most schools does not encourage this kind of practice. The Reflective Recess in Figure 3.1
asks you to reflect on your school organization and the issues that
are posed in this chapter.

Reflective Recess

1. What aspects of your work environment would you like to
   challenge?
2. What aspects of work do you believe your organization
   members would like to challenge?
3. How congruent are the responses in the previous questions?
4. How much energy and effort have you directed toward the
   following?
   a. Examining policies and practices that promote power and
      diminish powerlessness
   b. Developing networks and relationships within and outside
      of school for yourself and your constituents
   c. Establishing viable patterns of communication among and
      between constituent individuals and groups
5. What is your agenda, dream, or passion?
6. What absolutely enthralls or absorbs you about your work
   and your life?
7. What do you envision as an ennobling future for your organization?
8. What can you do to encourage this future?

Figure 3.1. Reflective Recess: Creating Empowering Cultures

I hope this exercise prompted you to consider the extent to which discrepancies exist between the rules, roles, and relationships in school and the quality of the work environment. Creating an empowering culture is not an easy task, nor is there any magic plan or formula. It requires committing on a long-term basis to continual improvement rather than achieving any one particular goal. Discovering and questioning new behaviors must be ongoing and focused on learning and practice. Envisioning schools as communities of learners and leaders means that the environment of work must be challenged—which in turn means that the prevailing norms of power and powerlessness, the kind of relationships within and outside of school, and patterns of communication must be questioned.

Conclusion

In order to adequately address the educational and social needs of students, we must address the needs of the adults in schools. The cycles of professional development are consonant with personal life cycles and development. Positive relationships, a sense of mastery, and developing a repertoire of skills play an important part in affirming ourselves. Contrary to this, painful beginnings and experiences can result in self-doubt and disengagement. Although the experience at work is related to an individual's capacity, much is related to the quality of life in the workplace. Consider this account of an individual as victim and the organization as villain:

I just had a discussion with a fellow educator who said that we work for the public and they are the boss, they pay us. And in that regard, he stated that we cannot fight the system but must go along with what the system wants. I find this very troubling. Perhaps this is why he and I do not see eye to eye on much in education. He stated that the system will get you. Hopefully, it has not gotten me. I still feel that I must fight for what I believe in my heart is right—for education and for my students. We have to take risks, we have to step outside the bounds of what has gone on before, we have to try and make a difference. Once we let the system get us, we have failed and we should get out of education. When I no longer think that I can make a difference, I need to leave. (L. H., personal communication, November 1992)

Those of us who value the institution of education should be concerned with the growth of people in schools. It is ludicrous to think of adult growth in schools as unrelated to student growth. For certain, differences among adults in schools are greater than among students. It is likely that we can make as many quantum leaps as our students, and it is equally possible that those leaps will not fall into some prescribed gender or time frame for such events.

Women's Example: Leadership and Learning Communities

There is no freeway to the future. No paved highway from here to tomorrow. There is only wilderness. Only uncertain terrain. There are no roadmaps. No signposts. So pioneering leaders rely upon a compass and a dream.

(JAMES M. KOUZES and BARRY Z. POSNER, *The Leadership Challenge*)

There is an abundance of literature devoted to discussing leadership yet little agreement on any particular or complete definition. I suppose leadership is somewhat like beauty or love—in the eye of the beholder, difficult to explain, but recognized because of its bewildering effect. Although some might view holding a position, office, or role as synonymous with leadership, this is not necessarily the case. Leadership in dynamic organizations and schools is a shared phenomenon. If we subscribe to the notion that virtually everyone has some potential for leadership, schools can be extraordinary places for expanding opportunities for leadership. We know that real leadership is the use of power not to dominate but to empower. This chapter discusses leadership and communities of learners. Leadership is considered in the contexts of teaching and learning, modeling and mentoring, and vision and reflection.

Leadership as Teaching and Learning

If we examine the traits associated with a leader, we find some similarity to those traits we would expect in an exemplary teacher—and how many good women teachers we have already in schools! A common thread in being a good leader, as in a good teacher, is having persistent interest in growth and development throughout life. Maurer (1991) suggests looking at leadership through frames of *values, vision, communication, teamwork, critical thinking, action,* and *self-confidence*. Good leaders and good teachers have a passion for compassion and an unyielding integrity that engenders trust. Their vision is well-developed and articulated with respect to what school is all about. They listen and exchange not only information but ideas and feelings. They inspire and promote teamwork among others and empower others through influence and responsibility. Problems are seen through multiple lenses. Understanding, serving as an example, patience, and persistence are critical attributes, and their confidence is evident in the way they share credit with others, in the way they take risks, and in the way they maintain a sense of humor.

The integrity of any institution is directly associated with the dignity of the individuals in that institution. Without trust, there is little integrity or dignity. Although there are enormous amounts of untapped human resources and opportunities in school for professional growth, many staff development experiences in schools are insulting to those who are most capable and have little relevance for those who are less capable. As Barth (1990) notes, this is closely related to the kind of relationships that exist within schools and how the principal functions as the catalyst.

Many teachers are not comfortable with "intruders" in the classroom nor do they view staff development as meaningful and relevant. There are exceptions, of course. However, as Lortie (1975) concluded,

For most teachers, learning, success, and satisfaction come largely from students within their classrooms. All other persons (parents, principal, teachers) without exception are connected with undesirable occurrences. Other adults have potential for hindrance, but not for help. (p. 169)

Sustained effort toward enhancing the professional growth of adults in schools will not necessarily result in immediate transformation. Adults vary as much as children in how they learn, when they learn, and under what conditions they learn. When the culture of the school is collaborative and collegial, it is highly likely that participation in professional development activities will be more than a matter of institutional compliance. Moreover, most programs support individual learning rather than collective or group learning.

It is one thing to teach someone a particular skill, such as a jump shot in basketball, but if never used in context or in concert with others (such as playing the game with teammates), the skill has little meaning. If learning is viewed only as *acquiring* certain knowledge and skills but not using them, this is translated into how we teach and lead. We must question not only traditional models about teaching and learning but also the appropriateness of categorizing adults in schools in leadership classifications. Senge (1990) suggests that the role of leaders in learning organizations lies in the responsibility for creating conditions in which people expand their capabilities to shape their future. This goes beyond just permitting people to pursue things that are important; it extends to encouraging and supporting these pursuits. Modeling and mentoring are powerful ways to increase personal capacity and, therefore, organizational capacity.

Modeling and Mentoring

Those who have discussed or written about their personal success point to the significance of role modeling and mentoring. Generally, women have had fewer women as role models and have been mentored less than men for certain leadership positions. Further, the leadership behavior and attitudes of those who might serve as role models in schools are often contrary to basic values and beliefs held by women about leadership and learning communities. I can think of many times when members of school faculty have been disappointed and critical of the fact that the principal was never in attendance at staff development sessions. The point seems a valid one, even with respect to the number of tasks and lack of time that principals may have. And this doesn't even begin to address the modeling by superintendents or board members as learners.

We become very frustrated with the routine of practice in schools. Principals, and others in positions of leadership, must come to understand the enormous influence there is in modeling the behavior they expect of others. Some things may have to be put aside or assigned a different priority. Here is another area where women have much to offer. Expanding the repertoire of leaders as learners has a profound impact on the quality of life in schools. It has always been distressing to me when I hear my students respond with statements such as, "I'm just a teacher." This is a powerful statement; yet, even though everyone might be capable of leading, it does not necessarily mean everyone wants to lead.

In part, I believe that the reticence to take on leadership responsibilities is because of how those in positions of leadership have presented themselves and been perceived. The typical organization of schools is not amenable to possibilities in differentiating roles, and much of our thinking is bounded by tradition. Also, and sadly so, those who take on added responsibilities seem to be rewarded by having more and more responsibilities placed on them. This does little to create schools as communities of learners and leaders. Modeling and mentoring can take on new definitions here, not in terms of roles but in terms of functions. Real leaders demonstrate what is important by how they set priorities, what they do and how they do it, and how they spend their time. Others make mental notes of these things.

Those who function as role models, consciously or otherwise, are not necessarily seen as mentors. We can choose to mentor someone but, as educators, we are in very visible positions and everything we do or say models some behavior. The greatest gifts we can hope to give are new and more positive ways of seeing the possibilities in others. Wisdom comes from having lived and having thought deeply about what we are all about in relationship to others. The place of models and mentors is so important in schools that opportunities must be expanded for drawing on this wealth of knowledge and experience. Our own and others' experiences are powerful ways of learning. Consciously seeking other kinds of experiences improves and enlarges our capacity to learn and to lead.

If we subscribe to the notion that real learning comes from doing, releasing the potential for individuals to derive meaning from experience is critical. People want a chance to do things that make them feel good about themselves, to accomplish things that are worthwhile, to learn new things, to develop new skills, and to do what they do best. Good leaders create meaning in a common cause through vision and reflection.

Vision and Reflection

The implied assumption that accompanies any discussion about vision is that the responsibility for forming and communicating a vision rests on an individual in a leadership position, such as a principal or superintendent. However, some would suggest that collective visions emerge from individual visions and evolve over time. In this respect, individual and organization visions are dynamic. When we imagine something extraordinary, beyond the ordinary in schools, it may likely be seen as idealistic. Yet, as Senge (1990) suggests, this can become the creative tension that drives organizations to greater growth and understanding.

Creative tension is the gap between our vision of where we want to be and the current reality of where we are. This tension can be resolved by lifting current reality toward the vision—or by lowering the vision toward reality. When vision and reality are on the same plane, however, organizations are static and there is no growth. The picture of "what might be" must be held in greater esteem than "what is." This is not to say that the current reality is to be ignored but that the motivation to change comes from a vision that confirms growth as generative rather than restrictive. Likewise, the focus is on seeing the systemic nature and the source of problems rather than symptoms. Both of these aspects of vision are already in place within the women in schools.

When we began as educators, we had some personal vision about our classroom or our school. Then, as Barth (1990) relates,

> By about December of our first year, something devastating and apparently inevitable begins to happen. Our personal vision becomes blurred by the well-meaning expectations and lists of others. Superintendents, state departments of education and universities often all but obliterate the personal visions of teachers and principals with their own abundant goals and objectives. The capacity to retain and adhere to a personal vision becomes blunted by exhaustion and compliance. It becomes too painful to have what we care deeply about repeatedly violated or discounted. So, our visions take refuge way down in our hip pockets where, in too many cases, they forever languish rather than inspire. (pp. 148-149)

It seems apparent that if we do not have a vision, a mental image of where we wish to be, we simply invite the imposition of others' visions on ourselves. Vision alone will not get us where we want to be. The creative tension caused by the distance between reality and vision must ebb and flow. Likewise, the relationships between people in schools must be synergistic. If visions are to be malleable in essence and firm in conviction, we must reflect on our actions and behaviors in light of what we have established as our vision. Our vision must be articulated and justified based on its educational soundness. We do far too much in schools that has little merit or worth.

A vision of school as a community of leaders, teachers, and learners recognizes the importance of seeing obstacles as opportunities. There must be genuine *commitment to goals*. People in schools need to be involved in establishing agendas rather than supporting others' agendas. *Adequate rewards, feedback, skills,* and *information* must be considered if significant modifications are to be made in the power structures of schools. Understanding schools as communities is a precondition to strengthening collegial relationships and fostering a culture of reflection and collaboration.

Figure 4.1 is a Reflective Recess that asks you to consider some of the issues just discussed. What responses caused you to wonder if you are doing only what works rather than what matters? What did you find about your organization that suggests that teaching, learning, and leading is the critical factor around which all else revolves?

Reflective Recess

1. How does your school or organization encourage learning for members?
2. Of your behaviors and actions, which would you wish for others to emulate?
3. Whom have you been a role model for?
4. Whom have you mentored?
5. Who has been a mentor for you?
6. To what degree is your school or organization a community of teachers, learners, and leaders?
7. What is the fundamental vision for your school or organization?
8. How great is the creative tension between vision and current reality?
9. What do you see as the vision in the following statement?

Our goal is to acknowledge the rich past and to develop a responsible and self-sufficient citizenry who possess the self-esteem, initiative, skills, and knowledge to continue learning throughout life. We value diversity, celebrate change, and affirm tradition.

Figure 4.1. Reflective Recess: Leadership and Learning Communities

Conclusion

This chapter focuses on the nature of leadership as teaching and learning and reminds us that women achieve the simultaneous combination of these qualities quite naturally. The importance of providing sustained professional growth for all adults in schools is underscored. Those in positions of leadership must be concerned with what models are presented in their actions and behavior.

Modeling and mentoring are powerful issues in the continuing growth and development of adults in schools. Embracing individual visions in the creation of a collective vision that evolves over time is a benchmark of schools as communities of learners and leaders.

I am reminded of a poem about the flight of geese. The essence of it was this: One day, a person lying on a lawn looked up to see geese flying gracefully in the formation of a V. Suddenly, yet rhythmically, the head goose swerved out and another promptly took its place. The goose that had been the leader took its place at the back of the line, and the formation was complete (Stomberg, 1982, p. 1).

I would imagine that, for the geese, it matters little whether the leader is goose or gander. Further, I would imagine that through collective effort there is greater distance to be gained than through the effort of a single goose charting a course alone.

Annotated Bibliography and References

Annotated Bibliography

Barth, R. (1990). *Improving schools from within: Teachers, parents, and principals can make a difference.* San Francisco: Jossey-Bass.
Roland Barth discusses how teachers, principals, and parents can be the most powerful source of ideas for changing our schools. From his many years in education, Barth shows how communication, collegiality, and risk taking among adults in schools can create an environment that encourages learning and leadership by all. He focuses on improving the relationships of adults inside and outside of schools.

Bolman, L. G., & Deal, T. (1993). *The path to school leadership: A portable mentor.* Newbury Park, CA: Corwin.
A quick-reading but thoughtful book which will help school leaders see troublesome situations in more creative ways, anticipate trouble before it arises, and develop more comprehensive and powerful strategies for leadership. This book in the "Roadmaps to Success" series is written as a lively dialogue between a seasoned veteran and a new administrator.

Cushner, K., McClelland, A., & Stafford, P. (1992). *Human diversity in education: An integrative approach.* New York: McGraw-Hill.

In this text, the authors offer an integrated approach to issues and experiences of human diversity drawn from the perspectives of anthropology, psychology, and sociology. They stress processes of cultural learning, how individuals become group members, and how cultural frameworks play into understanding and interacting with those who are different.

Goodlad, J., Soder, R., & Sirotnik, K. (Eds.). (1990). *The moral dimensions of teaching.* San Francisco: Jossey-Bass.

Goodlad, Soder, and Sirotnik put together essays in policy and philosophy on issues of teacher professionalism, moral responsibility, accountability, and ethics for the purpose of renewing civic and professional dialogue about educational dilemmas.

Levine, S. (1989). *Promoting adult growth in schools: The promise of professional development.* Boston: Allyn & Bacon.

Levine presents a guide to understanding the relationship between adult growth and professional development. She gives us a unique look at the real-life experiences of four teachers and how an understanding of developmental theory can encourage learning and growth. Commentary and reactions from teachers and administrators are included, which enrich the discussion.

Sarason, S. (1990). *The predictable failure of educational reform: Can we change the course before it's too late?* San Francisco: Jossey-Bass.

Sarason examines the reason that past attempts at reforming schools have failed and provides new perspectives on how reform must be undertaken if we expect to see successful resolution of the dilemmas that face schools. He argues that the aims of reform need to be reevaluated in light of how we foster the desire for lifelong learning. Sarason illustrates how the structure of schools is preserved in self-interest and power relationships.

Sarason, S. (1993). *Letters to a serious education president.* Newbury Park, CA: Corwin.

Using the form of letters to the first president of the 21st century, Sarason distills the wisdom and insights gained from his long career. His pivotal point is that "we must teach children, not subject matter," and to do so, we must start with "what and

*where children are." The letters are filled with concrete recom-
mendations and help the reader distinguish between issues that
are central and those that are secondary, or irrelevant.*

Sergiovanni, T. (1991). *The principalship: A reflective practice perspective.* San Francisco: Allyn & Bacon.

*The author utilizes reflective practice as a central theme in cre-
ating ways that administrators can resolve problems in practice. He suggests that administrators must explore mindscapes
that are congruent with the landscapes of their schools.
Sergiovanni discusses the nature of reflective practice, leadership and success, the mission of schooling, the development of
human resources, teaching and supervision, and moral dimensions of leadership.*

Sergiovanni, T. (1992). *Moral leadership: Getting to the heart of school
improvement.* San Francisco: Jossey-Bass.

*Sergiovanni argues that emotion, intuition, connection with
community, and moral authority are values that differ from the
rational and dominant thinking about leadership.*

Shakeshaft, C. (1989). *Women in educational administration.* Newbury Park, CA: Sage.

*Shakeshaft's book presents what has been learned about women
in educational administration. She includes a discussion about
too few women for too long, women's profiles and career paths,
barriers to advancement, and the androcentric bias in administrative theory and research. Comparisons and contrasts
are made between the way men and women lead schools in light
of the female world and school administration.*

References

American Association of School Administrators (1990). *Women and
minorities in school administration: Facts and figures 1989-1990.*
Arlington, VA: AASA.

Barth, R. (1990). *Improving schools from within: Teachers, parents, and
principals can make a difference.* San Francisco: Jossey-Bass.

Bernard, J. (1981). *The female world.* New York: The Free Press.

Biklen, S. (1985). *Can elementary school teaching be a career? A search
for new ways of understanding women's work.* Paper presented at

the annual meeting of the American Educational Research Association, Chicago.

Burbules, N. (1986). A theory of power in education. *Educational Theory, 36*(2), 95-114.

Cushner, K., McClelland, A., & Safford, P. (1992). *Human diversity in education: An integrated approach.* New York: McGraw-Hill.

Erikson, E. (1968). *Identity, youth and crisis.* New York: Norton.

Fullan, M. (1992). Getting reform right: What works and what doesn't. *Phi Delta Kappan, 73*(10), 745-752.

Gilligan, C. (1982). *In a different voice: Psychological theory and women's development.* Cambridge, MA: Harvard University Press.

Glickman, C. (1990). *Supervision of instruction: A developmental approach.* Boston: Allyn & Bacon.

Goodlad, J. (1983). *A place called school.* New York: McGraw-Hill.

Kohlberg, L. (1984). *The psychology of moral development.* San Francisco: Harper & Row.

Kouzes, J., & Posner, B. (1987). *The leadership challenge.* San Francisco: Jossey-Bass.

Lightfoot, S. (1983). *The good high school: Portraits of character and culture.* New York: Basic Books.

Loevinger, J. (1976). *Ego development: Conceptions and theories.* San Francisco: Jossey-Bass.

Lortie, D. (1975). *Schoolteacher: A sociological study.* Chicago: University of Chicago Press.

Maurer, R. (1991). *Managing conflict: Tactics for school administrators.* Needham Heights, MA: Simon & Schuster.

Ortiz, F., & Marshall, C. (1988). Women in educational administration. In N. Boyan (Ed.), *Handbook of research on educational administration.* New York: Longman.

Rizvi, F. (Ed.). (1987). *Educative leadership in a multicultural community.* Sydney, Australia: NSW Department of Education.

Sarason, S. (1990). *The predictable failure of educational reform: Can we change the course before it's too late?* San Francisco: Jossey-Bass.

Schein, E. (1985). *Organizational culture and leadership.* San Francisco: Jossey-Bass.

Senge, P. (1990). *The fifth discipline: The art and practice of the learning organization.* New York: Doubleday Currency.

Sergiovanni, T. (1991). *The principalship: A reflective practice perspective.* Boston: Allyn & Bacon.

Shaef, A. (1985). *Women's reality.* Minneapolis, MN: Winston Press.

Shakeshaft, C. (1989). *Women in educational administration.* Newbury Park, CA: Sage.

Stomberg, R. (1982). *The goose.* Unpublished poem.